GUITAR EXERCISES

10x Guitar Skills in 10 Minutes a Day

An Arsenal of 100+ Exercises for All Areas

-Guitar Head

GH@theguitarhead.com

www.facebook.com/theguitarhead/

and are the owned by the owners themselves, not affiliated with this document.

Disclaimer

Please note the information contained within this document is for educational and entertainment purposes only. Every attempt has been made to provide accurate, up to date and reliable complete information. No warranties of any kind are expressed or implied. Readers acknowledge that the author is not engaging in the rendering of legal and financial, medical or professional advice. The content of this book has been derived from various sources. Please consult a licensed professional before attempting any techniques outline in this book.

By reading this document, the reader agrees that under no circumstances are is the author responsible for any losses, direct or indirect, which are incurred as a result of the use of information contained within this document, including, but not limited to, - errors, omissions, or inaccuracies.

Guitar Head Bonuses!

Overdelivering! The one principle that all Guitar Head books are built around! From the very pricing of the book to the tons of bonuses offered, I want to make sure that you receive *10 folds the value* of the money you spent to buy this book! I genuinely want to help you master the guitar and I intend on doing this by providing immense value for the smallest price possible!

Follow the link to get your bonuses >> www.theguitarhead.com/bonus

Here is a list of all the things you'll find in the bonus section:

Book Specific Bonuses:

1. **Audio Tracks:** Not everyone are experts in reading tabs, a little extra help with the licks in the book can take you a long way. Hence, this book comes with backing audio tracks for EVERY lick in this book. Not only have I created supporting tracks for every lick in the book, but they are of *absolute high quality* with actual drums, various effects and various speeds for every track.

Other Bonuses:

2. **A Free Book:** Guitar mastery is all about nailing those small elements and avoiding mistakes. To make sure you don't make any of these common mistakes, I explain 25 common mistakes guitarists make and provide ways to avoid. I am giving it for free, you might as well go get it.

3. **Access to a private community of passionate guitarists:** Being around like-minded people is the first step in being successful at anything! The Guitar Head community is full of passionate guitarists who help each other excel! When you buy a Guitar Head book, you automatically become a part of this amazing community of people who are willing to listen to your music, answer your questions or talk about anything guitar! DO NOT MISS OUT ON THIS OPPORTUNITY – IT'S FREE! Sign up using the link provided and I'll send you mail giving access to the community!

4. **Free content delivered right to you:** When you sign up using the above link, you'll receive valuable guitar lessons delivered right to you! All you need to do? – Sit back and enjoy the content as you become a *Guitar God!*

5. **Entertainment and Guitar news:** Want to be in touch with the latest news and guitar content? Never miss out on a funny guitar video or interesting new development in the Guitar industry!

6. **A Lots more coming soon:** A lot more bonuses are in work, you can get a list of all the bonuses in works on my website and even *request bonuses!* A guitar glossary, a guitar road map, guitar wallpapers, free guitar music and lots more are in the works!

7. **All future books for free:** Yup! You read that right! I'm giving away all my future books for free in addition to exclusive access and special discounts for all future Guitar Head products! But there is a catch to this! I'm providing this exclusive benefit only to a select group of people. Want to know how you can get access? Keep reading, I have details about it somewhere in the book! I have placed the details at a random page of the book to filter out those who are not committed!

Quite a handful of bonuses, eh? These are the bonuses available at the time of release of this book. There might a ton more bonuses available depending on the time you are reading this. I am constantly adding new items to the list! So, make sure you grab your bonuses before moving on!

I can easily charge money for all these bonuses! But I genuinely want to help you achieve your goals! Money can come later!

You would be crazy to miss out on such an offer!

Follow the link to get your bonuses >> www.theguitarhead.com/bonus

Want to have a personal chat?

Want to have a personal one on one chat with me? I love connecting with my readers. Feel free to hit me up on my Facebook page or send me an email at *GH@theguitarhead.com*

Quick Tip:

Hey, did you know you can get the kindle version of this book for free? I have Amazon matchmaker enabled on all my book which enables you to get the kindle version for free if you purchase the paperback version.

I Can't Read Guitar TABS

Learning guitar without learning to read tabs is very much like crossing a busy road - blindfolded!

What do you do when you can't read? – You learn the alphabets.

What do you do when you can't count? – You learn the numbers.

What do you do when you can't read tabs? – You leave an offensive 1-star review on the book and you'll wake up the next day having complete knowledge on how to read tabs! (I'm just kidding – but disturbingly, that's what a few reviewers did!)

I understand if you are a beginner and can't read tabs; every person who can play the guitar has gone through that, including me. But the solution is not to get angry at the author and trash him in the review section. That's like saying "I want to learn to drive but I won't learn to read the street signs, I'll throw a stone at a cop instead!"

I feel sad for such people! They are missing out on such vital information! Learning to read guitar tabs won't take more than 30 minutes of your time and is very essential skill to have if you are learning guitar! Every guitar site, video or book on the internet communicates through written tabs and it is one of the first steps I teach in my students and in my book "Guitar for Beginners".

So, if you don't know to read tabs, I urge you to learn it before you take another step into the book. To make it easier for you, I wrote a whole book dedicated to reading tabs! It will teach you everything you need to know about reading tabs! And what's better - it is priced at a very nominal rate! You don't need to break a sweat!

You can get it here:

Amazon.com - https://amzn.to/2LjO3kR

Amazon.co.uk - https://amzn.to/2J8l2fi

I don't want to buy another book to use this book!

Now, this is a full-sized book with advanced instructions, exercises, audio back up and much more! It took me almost a month to create. That's the reason it is up for sale on amazon. It supports me and encourages me to create more awesome books for you!

If you are on a tight budget or if you are not in the mood to spend on another book, it's totally fine! You can follow the below link and download a PDF copy of the book for **FREE**. It contains everything that the paid version contains, you won't miss out on anything!

www.theguitarhead.com/tabs

Go ahead and download it! No hard feelings! :)

With your new-found tab reading skills and the free audio tracks that come with this book, I can already see you crushing the licks inside! Have fun!

Table of Content

12

Chapter #1

How to Use This Book

(Do not skip this)

Guitar exercises are something many guitarists don't enjoy as much as jamming to their favorite songs. I don't blame them; guitar exercises are often the boring, routine 1-2-3 exercises that you have been doing from the very first day you picked up a guitar. This book is here to change that - to make guitar exercises fun and compelling. With over 110 different FUN exercises, you will never be bored again.

Guitar exercises are crucial. They are specific and targeted at certain areas. For the sake of this explanation, let's say your bending skills are below average. While you can find a song with a lot of bending, the writer surely didn't write the song to help you improve your skills. It was meant to sound as good as possible. This is where depending on songs to improve your skills hits a stone wall. On the flip side, if you decide to increase the strength of your fingers by following a few exercises mentioned in this book, you will be way ahead of what you can expect from a song. You see, exercises are like missiles; you can enter the exact coordinates and the missile will go straight to the target in the most efficient way.

Here are some general tips and "how-to knowledge" to help you go through the book with ease.

What's inside?

This book contains 75 title exercises broken down into multiple smaller exercises, which brings us to around 110 exercises in total. Each exercise is my baby and has been built with specific areas in mind. That would explain the elaborate table of contents page giving importance to each exercise. Each exercise is special and, hence, given a unique name and tag. Special care has been taken to make sure that each exercise is unique and is to be found only this book.

The exercises in the book are arranged in an ascending order of their difficulty. Each exercise also contains a tag narrating the techniques involved, difficulty level, and category. This should make it easier for you to find the right type of exercise exactly when you need it.

The book is designed to entertain the beginners and the pros alike. As each exercise has its own tag, you may judge it before you give it a shot and make sure that the exercise is of your skill level. The skill level mentioned is a general indicator of difficulty and should not be considered for skipping exercises. An exercise that may seem advanced to you may, in actuality, be an intermediate exercise. So, I urge you to give each exercise a shot, even if you know for a fact that it's beyond your skill level.

I would also like to bring to your attention the fact that this book is purely an exercise book. I will not be teaching the various techniques involved. If you are interested in learning more on the techniques involved, feel free to email me at _GH@theguitarhead.com_. I would love to create more content for you.

You will not find huge descriptions for each exercise to bulk up the pages. The book is true to its name and will offer quality exercises along with necessary descriptions.

How do I use it?

A gym is a perfect metaphor for this book. The book contains various exercises such as bench press, chest press, barbell curl etc. Each exercise has been aimed at specific areas such as strength, stamina, speed, dexterity instead of chest, biceps or triceps. What you should do is repeat each exercise as many times as possible to build up each area. The more you can repeat, the better you get. If you feel you need to improve on your guitar speed, simply open up the speed section in the book and practice the exercises until you get your desired result.

The Magic of Every day

- Look for magic in your daily routine. – Lou Barlow

What you concentrate on, on a regular basis, grows. That's the mantra of every successful person out there. The same goes with guitar; practice every day and you will soon see results you never dreamed possible. Allow me to explain.

To bring my point out, let me introduce two imaginary characters - Richard and Ralph. Both love to play the guitar and both have regular jobs and families that keep them hopping all the time. To bring guitar into their routine, both come up with an action plan. Richard decides to play guitar for half an hour every day, as that's all the time he can spare in a working day.

Ralph, on the other hand, decides to play guitar every weekend for hours at a time.

Who do you think will become a better guitarist in the long run? If your guess was Richard, you are right!

Playing guitar is a skill that needs commitment and constant attention. It does not matter if you can only afford to spend 10 minutes a day on your guitar, you will be better than a person spending hours all at once when he finds time. Ten minutes every day is better than 2 hours on the weekend.

This is the difference I intend on making through this book. It does not matter if you are a professional guitarist or a beginner playing guitar as a hobby. If you are serious about this wonderful instrument, you should play at least 10 minutes every day.

You may surely practice more than 10 minutes a day, but I would like to keep our topic of discussion at 10 minutes to make sure that you get in the bare minimum.

How do I 10x my guitar skills?

Play every day! That's the mantra when it comes to guitar skills. Let's say you play half an hour a day; at least 10 minutes of the 30 minutes should be solely dedicated to guitar exercises.

Steve Vai, one of the greatest guitarists of all time, still does guitar exercises for an hour before he starts his practice session. He has made it a routine to work his fingers for an hour before his practice sessions. This is one of my objective through this book – to give you your very own personalised exercise routine.

Just like you would work out at a gym, pick out the area you would like to target each day and work your fingers to become a better guitarist. You may have a strength day, speed day, picking hand day, etc.

Follow a consistent routine for enough time and you will soon start noticing those gains! You will notice drastic improvements in your abilities as a guitarist.

Chapter #2

The Exercises are too Hard

I've had many people reach out to me saying the exercises in the book are too hard and I've had a few people lash out at me in the review section saying the exercises are too hard, the exercises don't make sense, don't bother with this book etc. Therefore I decided to have an entire chapter just to address this issue.

Now, I agree, some of the exercises inside the book might seem a little hard for a person starting out. But how is that a bad thing?

Getting out of your comfort zone

Everything you ever wanted is one step outside your comfort zone!

Pushing yourself to play things that are out of you level of comfort is how you progress with the guitar and in life. You can't expect to make considerable progress with the guitar if you only play things that you are comfortable with.

This book has NOT been designed to be completed in a day, rather, I see it as a companion throughout your guitar journey. From the very start of your journey to the day you feel you've covered a lot of ground on the fretboard – I want this book to be by your side! You can see the benefits of the book coming months and years from now. Trust me when I say this – there are a few exercises in this book that even I can't play without breaking a sweat, and *I wrote the book!*

If you are a beginner, I suggest you start with the exercises with the beginner tag and progress your way to the intermediate as you advance in your guitar journey! Surely you won't be bumping up levels today or tomorrow – it is a gradual process!

Break it down

While I have tried to break down all the exercises into bite-sized pieces that you can repeat over and over, if at any point you find an exercise difficult to play in one go, I would advise that you break it down into smaller bits and practice the bits over and over. You need not play the whole section in one shot. You will receive the same benefits if you do the exercise in one go or in pieces. The objective here is to make progress in improving on this skill and to have fun.

DO NOT try to play the whole exercise in one shot. Learn a bite sized part of the lick and practice it over and over until you feel you are making progress.

I hope you understand my mentality around this book. It is meant to be challenging, it is meant to push you beyond your limits, it is meant to be "not easy"!

I'm also working on a complete beginner's book for exercises, which should be out soon. So, stay tuned for that.

Take your time

This book contains around 110 exercises. While it could be exciting to finish all of them in one go, I would advise against it. First, the aim of the book is to build your different skill sets, such as accuracy, strength, stamina, etc. This requires a lot of repetition and practicing the same riff over and over again, until you feel the stretch in your hands. It is very much like working out in a gym – you do not want to cover all the equipment in one day. Ideally, what you should be doing is covering a few pieces of equipment, but in an organized and effective manner. That is how I want you to look at this book, as a group of equipment on which you should work systematically to see results.

Second, it can be very frustrating going through a lot of exercises in one shot. You have been warned, do not do that! I know, as when I was in the editing phase of the book, I had to play over all the exercises. While it is fun to play individual exercises, it can be very frustrating to play multiple ones at a time. The book is yours now and you can spend all the time you want with it. I would advise you to go through it slow and steady.

Chapter #3

Before You Start

- My guitar is not a thing. It is an extension of myself. It is who I am. –
Joan Jett

Just like you would do in a gym, stretches and warmups are essential to a good practice session with the guitar. Here are a few warmups and general stretches before we get into the meat of the matter.

Pre-Practice Relaxation

The first step to ensure a productive practice session is preparing the body to undertake the physical strains inherent to all guitar techniques. Contrary to popular belief, extensive stretching before playing might actually be counterproductive, rendering the still cold muscles and tendons weaker and more vulnerable to damage.

The best strategy is to gently warm-up your upper body, and eliminate all tension from your joints. Here are some steps you can follow to do so:

A

The neck and shoulder joints are at the core of proper posture and technique, overlooked stress in that area will have repercussions up to the tips of your fingers.

Start by standing up, arms loose and close to your body, then start by rolling your shoulders forward while gently opening and closing your hand for a minute; repeat, this time rolling your shoulders backwards.

B

Now slowly rotate your head in a clockwise and anti-clockwise motion, 30 seconds each.

C

Still standing up with your arms close to your body, raise your forearms to form a 90-degree angle at your elbows. While keeping your grip loose and hand straight, bend your wrist upwards and then back down for a minute; repeat, this time bending your wrist downwards.

This will warm-up the tendons in your forearm, the same tendons controlling the motion in your fingers.

String Skip Spider

Category: Fretting & Picking Hand

Techniques: String Skipping, Alternate Picking

(For anyone who skipped the initial pages of the book, I am providing free audio tracks that go along with the licks in this book, please refer the initial pages of this book to find out how you can get them)

Description: Spider exercises aim to work every finger in various combinations, but this one presents a little string skipping twist. It's a rarely encountered movement for the picking hand, and executing it accurately requires some adjustment time.

Economy of motion is paramount as always, however, to make the most out of the task, keep all pitches fretted for as long as you can, therefore working your stamina as well as your dexterity.

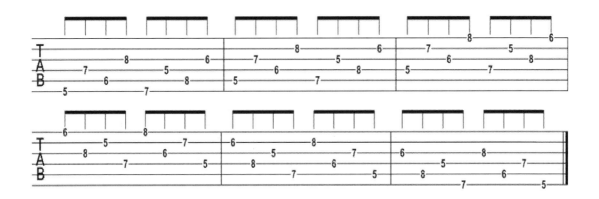

Eyes Wide Open

Category: Fretting & Picking Hand

Techniques: Finger Stretching, Sweep Picking/Fingerstyle

Description: Static effort can bear the same results as dynamic movement in a warmup routine. The wide chord voicings presented in this exercise promote blood flow in the fretting hand, while requiring the elimination of any excess stress or tension to be maintained.

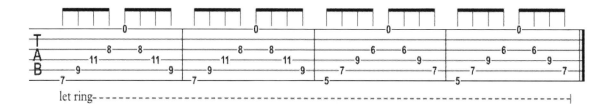

Slippery Slope

Category: Fretting Hand

Techniques: Legato

Description: A simple hammer-on/pull-off drill working all fingers. Proper legato execution requires a combination of raw strength and fine movement coordination, rendering it an excellent device to initiate a productive practice session.

26

A

B

Post-Practice Stretching

This section consists of a few basic stretches you would want to do after your productive practice session is complete. You can use some stretching routines to wind down and facilitate your recovery.

A

While standing up, raise your arms as far up as you can and maintain this position for ten seconds; now repeat, this time trying to touch your toes.

B

Stand in front of a wall and place your right palm on its surface with your fingers pointing up, keeping the arm straight, maintain for five seconds and repeat with your fingers pointing down; repeat for the other arm.

C

Now turn to your side and raise your arm to shoulder's height, placing your palm on the wall.

Get your body closer to the wall by slowly sliding your arm back, get as close to the wall as you can and hold for ten seconds; repeat with the other arm.

I Want You!

Are you a **passionate guitarist** with a burning desire to improve? Are you a guitarist who loves and appreciates the **magic six strings** can create?

And above all, did you absolutely **enjoy this book?** Would you like to see more such books?

If yes, I have an offer to make! I want to invite you to join the "*Passionate Few*" team. Every member of this team will receive **all future Guitar Head books for FREE!** You'll also receive special discounts and exclusive access to everything

Guitar Head has lined up for you! Sounds like a pretty good deal eh?

Click here to learn more >>

www.theguitarhead.com/passionate

Chapter #4

Play Better and Longer

- I don't need to speak; I play the guitar! - Joe Perry

Have you ever seen legendary guitarists play for hours together for thousands of people without breaking a sweat? They gig for hours together without thinking about it. This is because they've built the stamina to play for hours and the strength to keep that bend ringing.

This is what we will learn in this chapter – increasing your finger strength and stamina. I have created multiple exercises to target your finger muscles. There is going to be a lot of heavy lifting and legato in this chapter.

Let's get right into it, shall we?

Stir It Up

Category: Fretting Hand	
Level: Beginner	
Techniques: Legato	

Description: The premise of this exercise is fairly simple: targeting all possible finger combinations in a legato setting. Assigning a finger to each fret, ascend using hammer-ons and descend using pull-offs. Beware of the last combination as ring and pinky fingers are a weak combo, bring the metronome down if necessary.

A

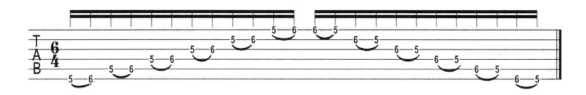

B

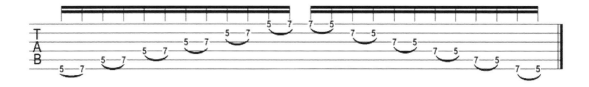

C

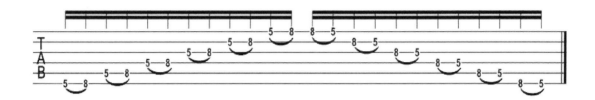

D

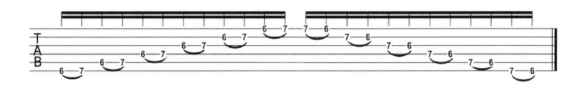

E

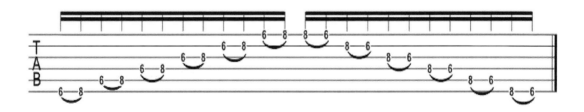

F

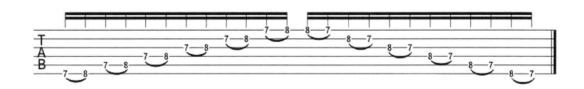

Burn The Page

Category: Fretting & Picking Hand		
Level: Beginner		
Techniques: Finger Roll, Alternate Picking		

Description: A tasty lick straight out of the arsenal of the best hard rock soloists of the 70s. It's an E Minor Pentatonic with some extra chromatic flare. To be played with an alternate picking style, emphasising the initial note of the pattern. Developing the finger roll necessary to consecutively play the same fret on two adjacent strings might take some time, take it slow at first and you'll be cranking that metronome in no time.

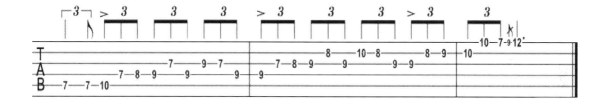

Double Shot

Category: Fretting & Picking Hand		
Level: Beginner		
Techniques: Alternate Picking, Finger Stretching		

Description: A three note per string G Major scalar run where every pitch is repeated twice; this allows the player to focus on economy of motion in the fretting hand while monitoring tension in the picking hand. Ensure adequate articulation of all notes and even dynamics throughout the pattern. Keep in mind that slow tempos bear as much challenge as the faster ones, as you will have to maintain a stretched position for longer.

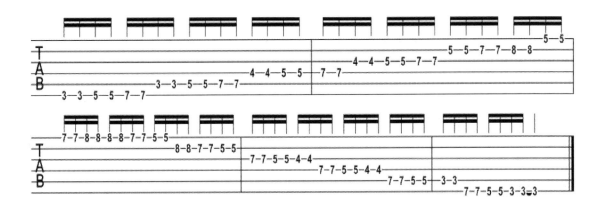

Ready Aim Fire

Category: Fretting Hand	
Level: Beginner	
Techniques: Bending	

Description: Bending strings can be a strenuous activity on the fingers, it stresses the wrist as well as the individual fingers and their skin. This exercise targets both pitch accuracy and endurance with a scalar pattern where the next diatonic pitch is reached by bending rather than fretting. Try it out with every finger, and make sure that the twisting motion comes from the rotation of the wrist, rather than vertical movement of the fingers themselves.

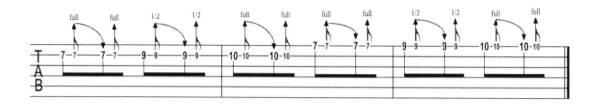

Cracking The Code

Category: Fretting Hand
Level: Beginner
Techniques: Legato

Description: In this legato routine the first finger acts as a pivot for the whole pattern, keep your index in place and let the note ring with confidence and uniformity throughout the exercise.

The pull-off motion of the third and fourth finger will require some dedicated work before seeing satisfactory results, just make sure not to strain your tendons as this is a delicate movement.

A

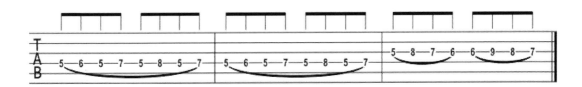

B

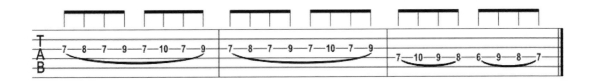

Laying The Groundwork

Category: Fretting Hand

Level: Intermediate

Techniques: Legato

Description: As simple as it gets. This exercise targets the development of hammer-ons and pull-offs through scalar application. Starting the pattern on the 3rd and 4th degrees of the major scale allows for the exploration of every finger combination you could encounter within its modes. There are a few unusual stretches lurking in the lick, you might want to be cautious!

A

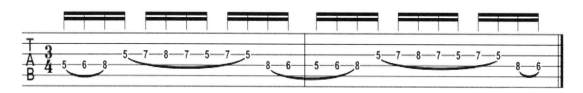

B

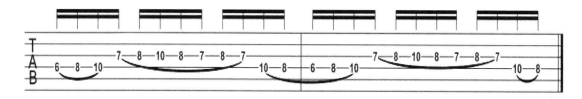

Shifting Logs

Category: Fretting & Picking Hand		
Level: Intermediate		
Techniques: Alternate Picking, Finger Stretching		

Description: This line presents a sequence of three note per string scalar patterns, but these are now moving horizontally rather than vertically. The position shift can be challenging at higher tempos, make sure to clearly outline the motion and not to lose alternation in the picking hand.

A

B

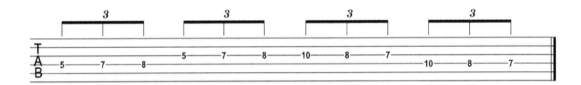

C

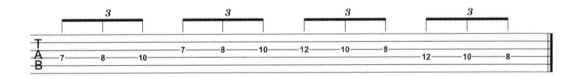

D

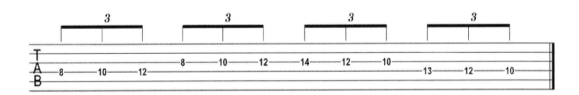

Bullets from Nowhere

Category: Fretting Hand	
Level: Intermediate	
Techniques: Hammer-ons from Nowhere	

Description: This exercise addresses finger strength through the technique of "hammer-ons from nowhere". Throw your pick away as your left hand will be doing all of the work this time, attack each note with a tapping motion, this will strengthen your tendons and improve their response time. It also works great for finger accuracy. Try out different finger combinations!

A

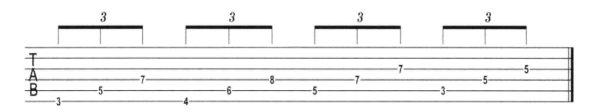

B

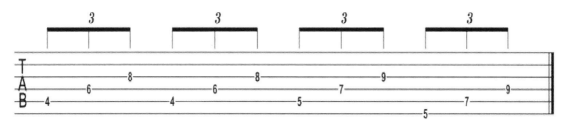

C

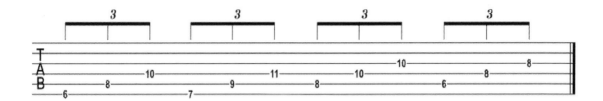

D

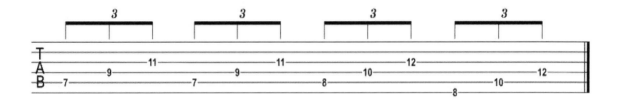

Close Encounters of the Third Inversion

Category: Fretting & Picking Hand

Level: Intermediate

Techniques: Alternate Picking, Position Shifting

Description: A Maj 7th arpeggio spanning three octaves, ascending and descending without losing consistency is a feat in resistance. Economy of motion is the key here, maintain a steady picking pattern while keeping your fingers as close as possible to the fretboard, smoothly shifting your fretting hand between positions. Try breaking it up into bite-sized pieces if you are having trouble nailing it in one go.

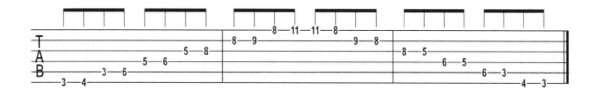

Trial by Fire

Category: Fretting & Picking Hand
Level: Intermediate
Techniques: Alternate Picking

Description: This neo-classical styled line is as simple as unforgiving, be aware of the proper articulation of each note, and the dynamics between the open string and the fretted pitches. This has to be one of my favorite riffs form this section. Just learn the frets involved and you can noodle away on any string!

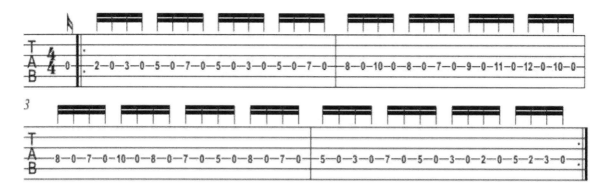

Out in The Open

Category: Fretting & Picking Hand
Level: Intermediate
Techniques: Downpicking, Economy Picking, Legato

Description: A melodic riff revolving around open chord positions. The first two bars require a mix of downpicking and economy picking to be performed, and the last two bars provide a rest for the picking hand, but call for the employment of hammer-ons and pull-offs involving open strings, so be careful!

A

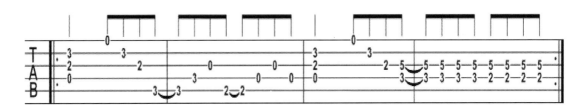

B

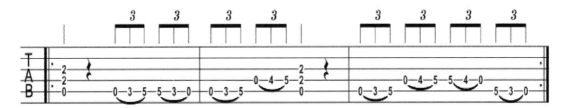

Chromatic Legato

Category: Fretting Hand		
Level: Advanced		
Techniques: Legato, Finger Stretching		

Description: Hammer-on and pull-off workout for every finger. Try to obtain a dynamic consistency throughout the pattern, especially when using weaker fingers. Sliding from one position to the next could be challenging in terms of timing, make sure to not to lose track of the subdivisions!

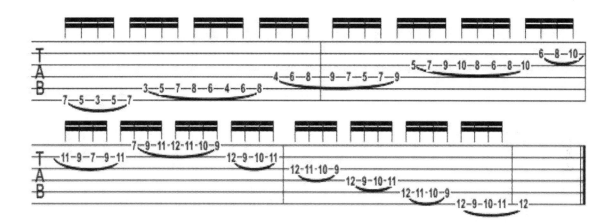

Crystal Cave

Category: Fretting & Picking Hand
Level: Advanced
Techniques: Finger Stretch, Fingerstyle

Description: When talking about left hand strengthening the first thing that comes to mind is some blistering scalar run across three octaves, but static tensions plays a major role in finger strength development. Hold these chords and arpeggiate them, trying to be as accurate as possible when changing position. Spread voicings can prove to be an effective warm-up strategy and stamina developing tool, just make sure not to strain your tendons.

A

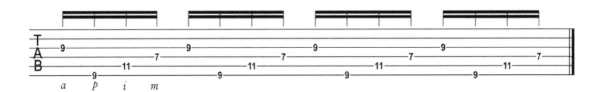

B

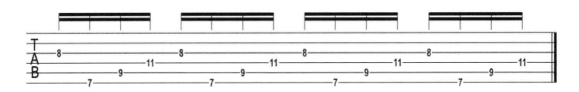

C

D

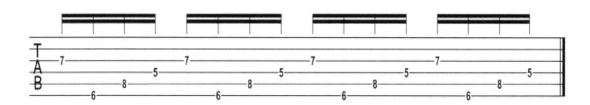

Spicy Neighbours

Category: Fretting & Picking Hand
Level: Advanced
Techniques: Alternate Picking, Economy Picking

Description: This lick constructed on the C Melodic Minor scale takes full advantage of chromaticisms to spice up its effect. Try different combinations of alternate and economy picking; a good strategy could be to alternate pick until the occurrence of the mini-sweep beginning on the "a" of the third beat, which would be economy picked, and then resume alternate picking.

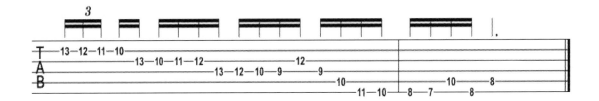

Attack!

Category: Fretting & Picking Hand		
Level: Advanced		
Techniques: Alternate Picking		

Description: This frantically aggressive modern rock riff targets your endurance through a series of wide movements in both the fretting and the picking hand. The 16th note triplets challenge both your timing and relaxation, and require complete familiarity with the phrase to be executed with confidence. Try palm muting the pitches played on the low E string which should add a percussive effect to the line.

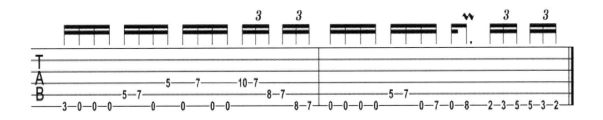

Chapter #5

Play Faster and Accurately

- My first love was the sound of guitar. – Boz Scaggs

"I wish I could play faster!" I am sure every guitarist out there has had this thought at least once on their guitar journey. Well, that's absolutely fine, doesn't everything sound better when played faster?

Through this chapter, I intend on helping you play faster. We will be aiming to increase our overall speed and dexterity in this chapter. From beginner level techniques to advanced techniques, you will notice a significant increase in your speed levels once you are through with this chapter.

As the saying goes - to play faster, you have to first go slow. This is why I have provided a speed you can start with and the speed you should aim for in the tags for this chapter. Your objective should be to gradually increase your speed until you hit the desired target. Don't forget – the slower you practice, the faster you get.

So, get your metronome out! Let's begin!

Chromasweep

Category: Fretting & Picking Hand
Level: Beginner
Techniques: Sweep Picking

Starting BPM: 45
Goal BPM: 80

Description: This exercise focuses on the fundamental motion of sweep picking by trimming it down to its smallest terms. The chromatic nature of the line will allow you to easily internalise the fret pattern and therefore direct your active attention to the movement itself.

Be aware of the resonating unused strings, use your right palm to mute the low E and A strings while lightly touching the high E string with your fretting hand fingers.

The motion of the pick should be continuously flowing; make sure to find a comfortable angle at which to hold the pick and don't change it throughout the movement.

A

B

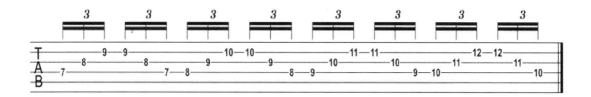

The Ascent

Category: Fretting Hand
Level: Beginner
Techniques: Hammer-On

Starting BPM: 50
Goal BPM: 80

Description: The building block of hammer-on exercises: the single string scale over a pedal tonic. It's simple in its premise, but requires some dedication to master. Don't get carried away and aim at cohesion and precision of attack throughout the phrase.

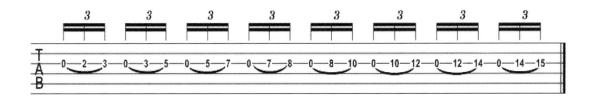

The Descent

Category: Fretting Hand	
Level: Beginner	
Techniques: Pull-Off	

Starting BPM: 40	
Goal BPM: 80	

Description: Once you've reached the peak, you've got to come down.

Slightly more challenging than it's hammer-on variation, this exercise will develop accuracy and strength calibration in your fretting hand; vital elements for a seamless execution of the pull-off.

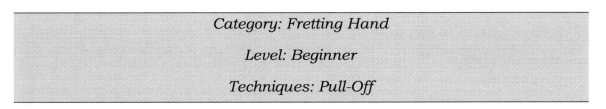

Fire in The Cabin

Category: Fretting Hand
Level: Beginner
Techniques: Hammer-On

Starting BPM: 100
Goal BPM: 150

Description: A brief ascending pentatonic pattern in the style of many rockers.

The hammer-on technique is well suited to blistering speeds, but dynamic consistency and articulation should always be your primary goal, so don't get tempted by cranking up the metronome straight-away, and listen to every nuance of the line!

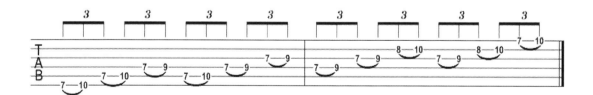

Fire in The Cockpit

Category: Fretting Hand
Level: Beginner
Techniques: Pull-Off

Starting BPM: 80
Goal BPM: 150

Description: The pull-off counterpart to the previous exercise. Much more challenging, as it requires greater finger strength and coordination to produce an accurate output.

Start slow and play your way up slowly but surely; this technique requires patience, practise it a little bit every day for better results.

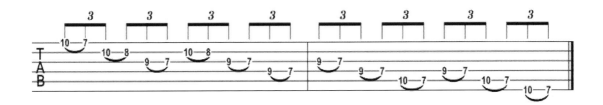

Eerie Sweeps

Category: Fretting & Picking Hand
Level: Intermediate
Techniques: Sweep Picking, Economy Picking

Starting BPM: 60
Goal BPM: 110

Description: This series of phrases is based on the fourth and fifth modes of B Harmonic Minor and combines the incorporation of the 6th in the arpeggios along with short scalar passages. The resulting pattern calls for the combined employment of sweep and economy picking to be properly executed. Always keep economy of motion in mind, and work out which fingering is best adaptable to your personal technique.

A

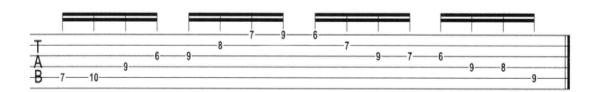

B

C

Three by Five

	Category: Fretting Hand	
	Level: Intermediate	
	Techniques: Finger Stretching	

	Starting BPM: 90	
	Goal BPM: 140	

Description: A very unorthodox approach to pentatonic playing: rather than opting for a two-note-per-string pattern, the third note is played on the same string and then repeated on the adjacent one. The result is a great finger stretching routine, bearing an interesting musical effect to incorporate in your playing.

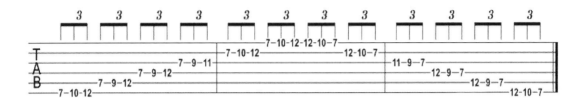

Just Tap Water for Me

Category: Fretting & Picking Hand
Level: Intermediate
Techniques: Tapping

Starting BPM: 80
Goal BPM: 130

Description: A well-executed tapping phrase will have sensational effects on a crowd but, while it might seem like a daunting technique at first, a little bit of consistent practice will go a long way. Get the basics down with these two phrases, the first one incorporating open strings and the second one being purely scalar.

For the tapped note you could either use your index or middle finger, experiment with both to find out which one comes more comfortable to you.

While the initial attack of the tap provides thrust to the pattern, the left-hand legato will maintain said thrust alive; ensure dynamic consistency and prevent adjacent strings from resonating.

A

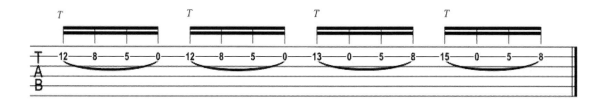

B

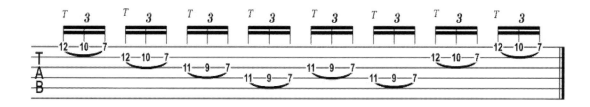

Peckin' Around

	Category: Fretting & Picking Hand	
	Level: Intermediate	
	Techniques: Legato, Chicken Picking	

Starting BPM: 75
Goal BPM: 115

Description: This brief pentatonic riff presents a few chromaticisms to provide some exercise to all four fingers. Attack the D string with your pick while plucking the G string with your middle finger. The hardest challenge of this line is evenness of articulation, especially considering the presence of the finger-roll in the third beat of the pattern.

Don't be afraid to keep a lower tempo until you've mastered the basic motion behind the exercise.

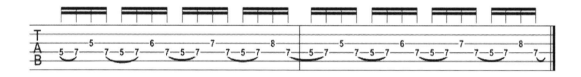

Ripples in The Water

Category: Fretting
Level: Intermediate
Techniques: Holdsworthian Legato, Economy Picking

Starting BPM: 60
Goal BPM: 110

Description: In this task we explore another kind of legato made famous by fusion player Allan Holdsworth. This technique avoids the use of pull-offs, making legato solely a tapping effort. Descending motions can prove particularly difficult, as they require lifting off the finger playing the higher pitch first and then tapping a lower note with another finger, relying on seamless coordination. However, the technique has its advantages, such as ease of transition between legato and other techniques, and general consistency of articulation.

As always, start at a comfortable tempo and only increase the mark when you're in full control of every note played.

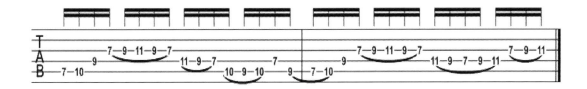

Seventh Seal

Category: Fretting & Picking Hand
Level: Intermediate
Techniques: Economy Picking

Starting BPM: 65
Goal BPM: 105

Description: Chained seventh arpeggios requiring position shifting and economy picking.

The addition of slide and legato passages eases the transition between positions, and adds some variation in texture.

Maintain a constant angle between the pick and the strings, relying predominantly on the wrist to carry out the motion, but slightly adjusting the forearm to accommodate the six string spread of the pattern.

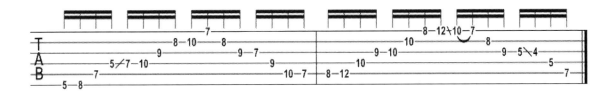

Sliding Over Steps

Category: Fretting Hand
Level: Intermediate
Techniques: Slide

Starting BPM: 70
Goal BPM: 130

Description: A cascade of ascending and descending diatonic slides targeting accuracy and dexterity. Working out the best fingering for the pattern can be tricky, consider every option while trying to make it sound as graceful and continuous as possible.

Treat it as a monophonic synth line, there should be no overlap between pitches and minimal string noise should be produced.

A

B

String Skip Legato

Category: Fretting Hand
Level: Advanced
Techniques: String Skipping, Legato

Starting BPM: 90
Goal BPM: 150

Description: An intricate scalar phrase, making full use of legato and string skipping.

Try parallel techniques such as chicken picking and Holdsworthian legato to give it a twist.

The biggest challenge of the pattern is reducing string noise down to a minimum while ensuring a consistent articulation of picked and slurred pitches.

Allow at least a week of practice at a moderate speed to internalise the movement, and increase the tempo gradually, without causing any strain to your tendons.

A

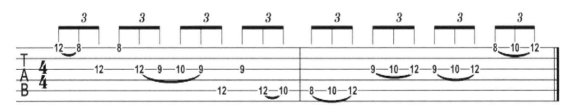

B

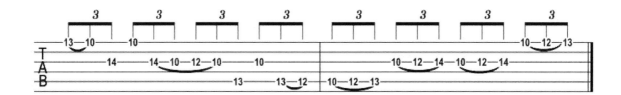

I'll Get a Lift

Category: Fretting & Picking Hand
Level: Advanced
Techniques: Legato, Chicken Picking, String Skipping

Starting BPM: 80
Goal BPM: 130

Description: These two phrases make unconventional use of scale boxes, incorporating string skipping to accommodate wider intervals, and using legato for ease of playability.

The initial attack of the notes is the most crucial element, assign your pick to the G string and your middle finger to the high E string, ensuring that the notes played on the latter are as intelligible as the ones played on the former.

A

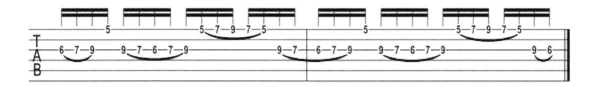

B

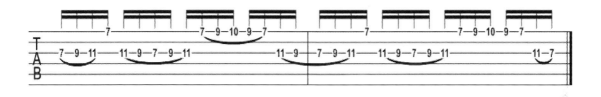

Trail Mix

Category: Fretting & Picking Hand
Level: Advanced
Techniques: Legato, String Skipping, Economy Picking, Slide

Starting BPM: 70
Goal BPM: 105

Description: This constant 16ths melodic phrase is a feat in coordination and accuracy.

It incorporates several techniques along with a position shift, requiring great care in articulation, dynamics, and economy of motion. Aim to produce a flowing and musical result without any stutter, decreasing the starting tempo if necessary.

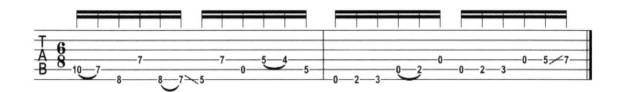

Chapter #6

Tame Your Picking Hand

- The guitar chose me. – Charlie Byrd

What do you do when you can't nail a solo or play a song the way it's meant to be played? You practice for hours, together, focusing on each and every fret you play. But what about your other hand? After all, you need two hands to be able to play well.

The Picking hand is probably the most ignored while learning guitar. It is expected to keep up with the fretting hand with no effort taken to concentrate and improve it. For all you know, you might be failing at playing what you want all because your picking hand is not good enough.

I am here to offer you a solution. A solution that will passively increase your guitar skills by targeting the most ignored part of your guitar journey.

Also, this chapter will not have a category section in the tags as all of them are aimed at the picking hand.

Starting The Engine

Level: Beginner

Techniques: Alternate Picking

Description: A series of exercises targeting the fundamentals of alternate picking, completely executed on open strings to allow you to focus solely on your picking hand.

Change of subdivision, odd groupings, even groupings, this task covers all the basics for having a productive start.

A

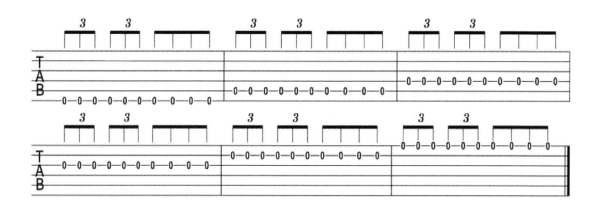

B

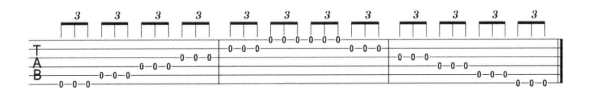

C

Pima Puma

Level: Beginner	
Techniques: Fingerstyle	

Description: Doesn't get much simpler than this. Put your pick on the side and let's get those fingers to work. Don't keep your wrist too close to the body of the guitar, as the motion should come from moving the metacarpal bones, and not by flexing the joints in a clenching fashion.

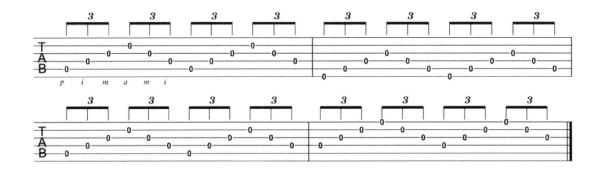

The Hen's Walk

Level: Beginner

Techniques: Chicken Picking

Description: This simple exercise targets coordination and facility with alternating between stroked notes and plucked ones. Always attack with a downstroke, and follow with a decise pop with your middle or ring fingers. The biggest challenge of this technique is to obtain a constant volume between both picked and plucked notes, try softening your pick attack as plucking too hard with your fingers might cause blisters to form.

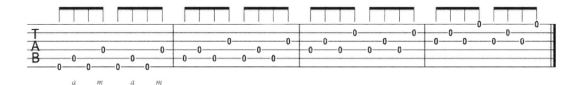

Three Feet Under

Level: Beginner
Techniques: Downpicking

Description: Downpicking can be a daunting technique, just a few minutes of intense practice can cause tension and discomfort in the wrist joint. Take it easy with some repeated pitch triplets, the fretting hand pattern is easy enough for you to concentrate on your picking hand relaxation. Maintain a consistent level of dynamics throughout, especially when changing strings.

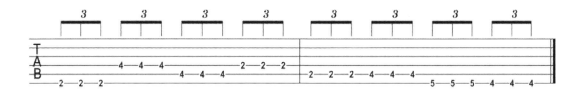

Bottom Up

Level: Intermediate

Techniques: Sweep Picking

Description: Try your sweep picking skills with a basic triadic progression on the top three strings. Only increase the tempo when the movement is in continuous flow, and all pitches are equally articulated. Sweep picking is one of those techniques that require patient practice for good results, spend a week or two just getting comfortable with the movement.

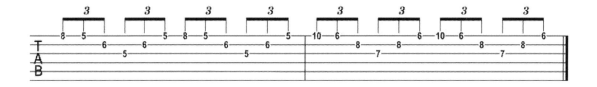

To The Sun and Back

Level: Intermediate

Techniques: Alternate Picking, String Skipping

Description: An ascending major scale where every pitch is alternated to the octave of the tonic. This requires a downstroke followed by an upstroke on another string, calling for a controlled and economic motion of the wrist. Experiment with pick angles, it really makes a difference.

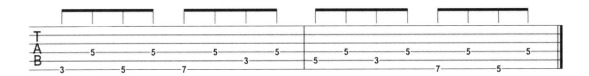

Jump The Rope

Level: Intermediate

Techniques: Alternate Picking, String Skipping

Description: A pentatonic lick with a twist, the wider intervals caused by string skip make for an interesting effect, but require particular coordination to maintain a flow and continuity throughout the pattern. Progressively move your forearm downwards as you get into the higher register.

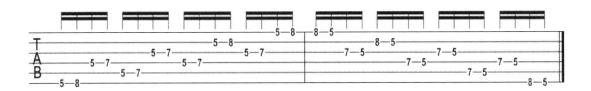

71

Economy 101

Description: A simple scalar phrase to test your economy picking. Always try and produce a single motion when playing two adjacent strings, the economy is lost if you break down the movement, you might go bankrupt!

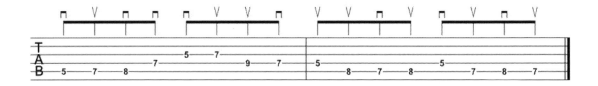

Middle Ground

Description: Now that you're at ease with the fundamentals of sweep picking, try and add another string to the sequence. You'll now experience the first instances of string noise, manage it with a combination of your picking hand's palm and you fretting hand's fingers.

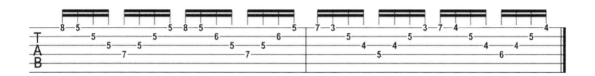

Soaring Waves

Level: Advanced

Techniques: Sweep Picking

Description: Same old progression, but now spanning a whopping five strings! String noise management is now paramount. You'll have to employ what is called "progressive palm muting", which is essentially lowering the side of your hand along the strings while you ascend. Try beginning the progression with an upstroke, it will allow you to ascend to the top with a single uninterrupted motion.

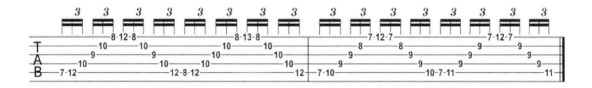

Chapter #7

Play Legendary Solos

- The guitar was my weapon, my shield to hide behind. – Brian May

Soloing! The best thing you can do on a guitar! You can noodle all day, replicate legendary solos, create your own style, the list is endless. In this chapter, we will tackle various scale patterns to help you nail that solo you have in mind!

We will tackle only scale exercises in this chapter. If you want to learn more about the technical aspects of scales and soloing, sign up for my newsfeed. I have a soon-to-be-released in-depth book on scales, which will teach you all you need to know about scales and mastering solos. You may download any of the bonuses on *www.theguitarhead.com/bonus* to be a part of the mailing list.

I might even give it away for free to those on my mailing list, so hurry! Sign up now!

Yin and Yang

Category: Picking & Fretting Hand
Level: Beginner
Techniques: Alternate Picking, Legato
Scale used: C Minor

Description: This exercise largely features the concept of opposites: an ascending triple followed by a descending one; a slurred triplet followed by fully picked one.

Learning single string scalar patterns enhances your understanding of the instrument, freeing horizontal rather than vertical movement.

A

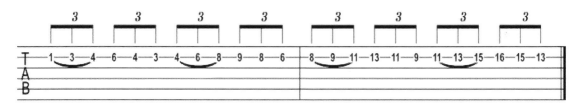

B

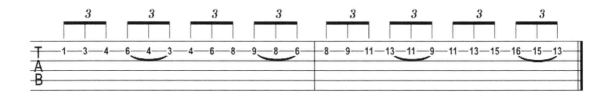

Just A Couple

Category: Fretting & Picking Hand
Level: Beginner
Techniques: Alternate Picking, Position Shifting
Scale used: A Minor Pentatonic

Description: A purely horizontal variation of the box shifts within the pentatonic scale.

In variation A, the four top notes of a box are played descending, before ascending to the next box, while in variation B the pattern is reversed. Try it with all couples of strings!

A

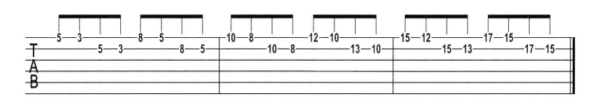

B

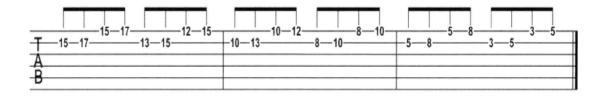

Rainy Morning

Category: Fretting & Picking Hand

Level: Beginner

Techniques: Alternate Picking, Finger Rolling

Scale used: E Dorian

Description: A simple melodic line based on the Dorian mode, it features the use of the finger roll in the Em11 arpeggio, as well as purely scalar passages, suggesting a further exploration of mixes of this kind to the player.

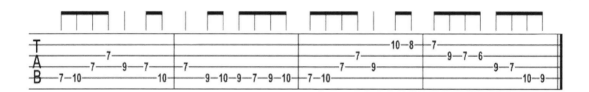

Sprints

Category: Fretting & Picking Hand

Level: Beginner

Techniques: Alternate Picking

Scale used: D Major

Description: A simple ascending and descending D major scale, alternating every two beats between 8th and 16th subdivisions. These speed bursts not

77

only target your tempo feel, but also help you improve your ability to manage the tendency to increase tension in the wrist when accelerating.

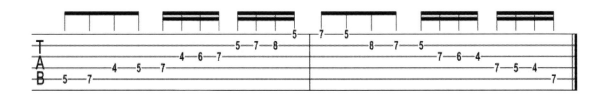

Car Chase

Category: Fretting Hand		
Level: Intermediate		
Techniques: Hammer-On		
Scale used: D Major		

Description: A blistering ascending scale pattern. It's easy forgo precision in hammer-ons only phrases, don't neglect your time, tone, and articulation when practising this exercise.

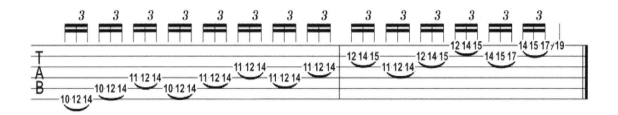

Just Perfect

Category: Fretting & Picking Hand
Level: Intermediate
Techniques: Alternate Picking, Finger Stretching
Scale used: G Major

Description: A simple succession of ascending perfect fifths spanning three octaves.

Two-note-per-string patterns do wonder for stamina and relaxation, and this exercise comes with the added benefit of a good stretching workout. Visualising and naming the notes on the neck will help you to break out of scale boxes, and in finding your way when soloing.

Cow Lick

Category: Picking Hand

Level: Intermediate

Techniques: Alternate Picking

Scale used: G Mixolydian

Description: This blues flavoured lick reminds you that open strings can be a strong ally even when your fretting hand is way up the neck! Always know the alterations of the key in which you're playing, this will tell you which open strings are diatonic to your tonality.

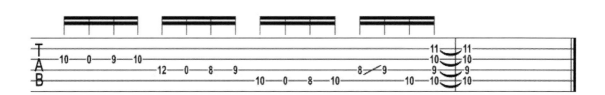

Enclosing Beasts

Category: Picking Hand

Level: Intermediate

Techniques: Alternate Picking

Scale used: B Minor

Description: However, not every note you play when soloing must be diatonic to the key, in this exercise we explore the technique called "enclosure", which is approaching your target note both from above and below. In this instance we are starting a diatonic step above the note, then briefly playing the target note before descending another semitone, then finally resolving again to the wanted pitch.

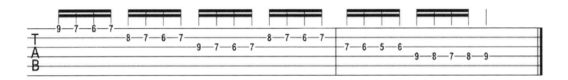

Passing By

Category: Fretting & Picking Hand
Level: Intermediate
Techniques: Economy Picking, Legato, Slide
Scale used: A Mixolydian

Description: The following phrase incorporates several techniques, and forces the player outside of the initial box, by using two adjacent major triads to shift position.

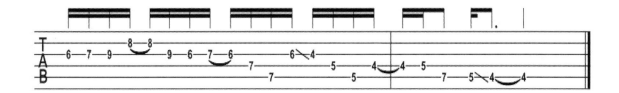

Move Those Boxes

Category: Fretting & Picking Hand
Level: Intermediate
Techniques: Alternate Picking
Scale used: A Minor Pentatonic

Description: A further exploration of horizontal shifts between the pentatonic boxes.

Beginning the new pattern on one of the pitches belonging to the previous box grants a certain continuity of sound, while allowing a greater reach up the instrument's neck.

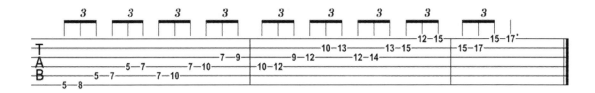

Internal Triads

Category: Fretting & Picking Hand
Level: Intermediate
Techniques: Alternate Picking, Economy Picking, Finger Stretching, Finger Roll
Scale used: G Major

Description: Triadic playing doesn't have to be purely chordal, individuating triads inside scale boxes will increase melodic control when soloing, and help outlining harmonic progressions. In variation A we see a sequence of ascending triads ascending up the scale, while in variation B a series of descending triads descending down the scale is played.

A

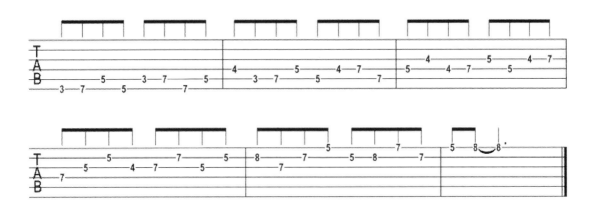

B

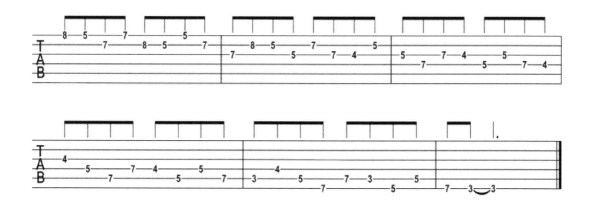

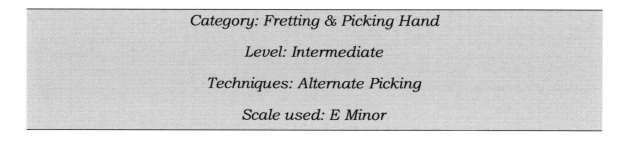

Three Trees

Category: Fretting & Picking Hand
Level: Intermediate
Techniques: Alternate Picking
Scale used: E Minor

Description: The following exercise aims to suggest a different way of visualising the scale.

Intervallic playing, rather than a purely sequentially diatonic style, can provide some "space" in one's solos. This pattern specifically explores the interval of a diatonic third, but feel free to experiment with other intervals!

A

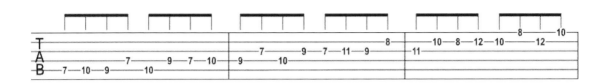

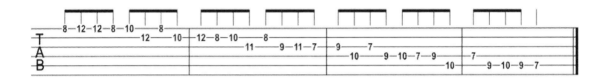

B

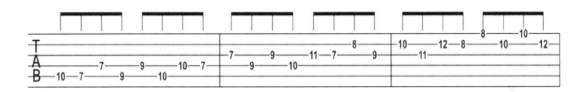

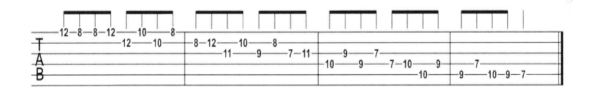

The Leap

Category: Fretting & Picking Hand	
Level: Advanced	
Techniques: Alternate Picking, String Skipping	
Scales used:	
A: F Dorian	
B: G Phrygian	
C: Ab Lydian	

Description: An effective way to instantly freshen up your playing is simply changing your perspective on what you already know. This exercise is based on simple three-note-per-string scalar patterns, but omits every other string, resulting in an interesting mix of diatonic steps and leaps. Keep a loose wrist in your picking hand, always monitoring string noise, and minimise motion in the fretting hand.

A

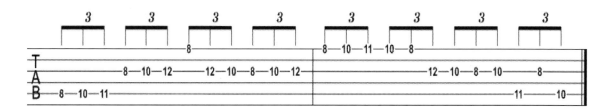

B

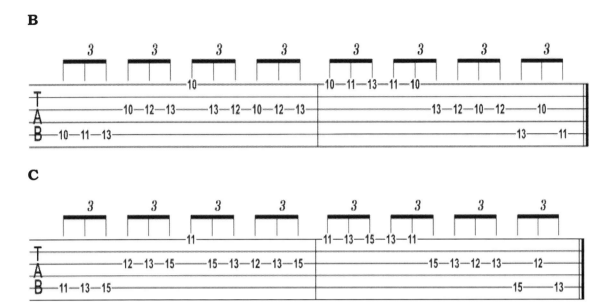

C

That Escalated Quickly

Category: Fretting & Picking Hand		
Level: Advanced		
Techniques: Economy Picking, Finger Stretching		
Scale used: A Minor Pentatonic		

Description: When soloing using pentatonics it's common to gravitate around sequential patterns or licks we know, but arpeggios and uneven groupings of notes can be an effective tool to spice up your pentatonic playing. In this exercise we use a 2-1-3 notes per string pattern to outline an Am7 and a C6 arpeggios, and then repeating them up the octave.

The employment of economy picking adds an element of fluidity, unusual for a pentatonic line.

Climbing Back Up

Category: Fretting Hand
Level: Advanced
Techniques: Pull-Off
Scale used: B Minor

Description: The follow-up to "Car Chase", it features a pull-offs based descending pattern.

The repeated groups of three on every string make the challenge more manageable, although dynamic consistency and clear articulations will only come with time.

Make sure to practice this exercise only when fully warmed up.

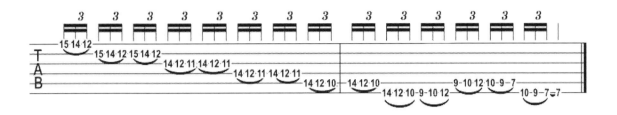

Chapter #8

Master Chords & Arpeggio

- All I have is this guitar, these chords and the truth. – Jon Bon Jovi

Beginner chords to chords with names longer than the song itself. Chords are everywhere! Mastering them is essential, irrespective of your level of skill.

Through this chapter, we will master chords and Arpeggios through a series of exercises designed specifically for the fretting hand. Let's dive in!

Through Stained Glass

Level: Beginner
Techniques: Economy Picking

Description: One wouldn't necessarily think of arpeggiated open chords as an economy picking exercise, but applying such technique in this context makes for an effortless and more fluid comping. Keep your wrist loose and distant from the strings, to shortening their natural sustain through muting.

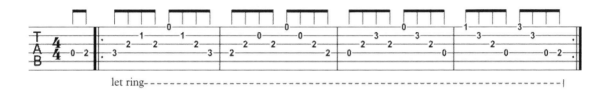

let ring--|

Raising The Barre

Level: Beginner

Techniques: Alternate Picking, Barre Chords

Description: Barre chords, as simple as they are, prove to be a valuable tool in the arsenal of every guitarist, and are incredibly useful as strengthening devices for the fretting hand as they engage all muscles in the hand and require consistency of grip for all strings to properly resonate.

Catch two birds with one stone by incorporating repeated 16th notes in the picking hand to develop relaxation and stamina in alternate picking.

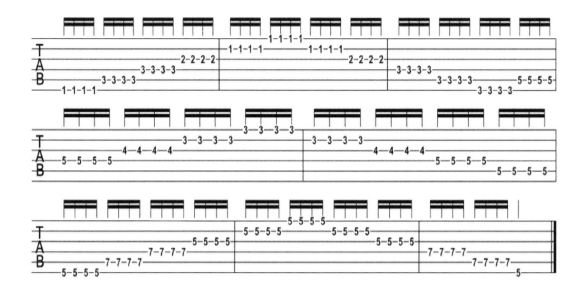

Chilling at Nine

Level: Intermediate
Techniques: Fingerstyle

Description: This exercise introduces the concept of independent bass movement through a simple ïi-I" progression suitable to a modal landscape. Pluck the upper structure of the voicings with your index, middle, and ring fingers, while executing the simple bassline on the bottom two strings with your thumb. Once you're comfortable with this basic tonic to dominant movement, you can introduce increasingly complex and independent accompaniments in the thumb.

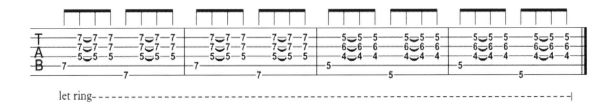

let ring- -|

Fresh Moves

Level: Intermediate

Techniques: Strumming, Ghost-Notes

Description: A driving funk rhythm part, featuring abundant syncopation and ghost notes.

Always outline every 16th subdivision with your picking hand, hovering over the strings when not playing; this constant motion will help you keep track of not only the metronomic time, but also what's referred to as "pocket", or how well your part rhythmically interlocks with the whole ensemble.

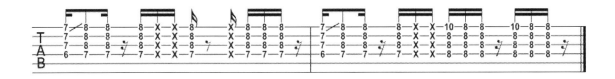

Suspension Bridge

Level: Intermediate	
Techniques: Strumming	

Description: A galloping succession of sus4 chords resolving to a major triad, these are a common harmonic device, especially useful when delaying resolution or building anticipation. The rhythmic subdivision, while simple, provides the player with a challenge in consistency. Always keep articulation and dynamics at the forefront of your practice.

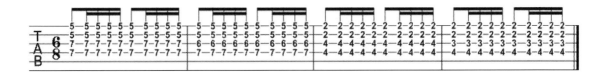

Sleepy Time

Level: Intermediate	
Techniques: Fingerstyle	

Description: A melodic bass part over a low-key arpeggiated triadic progression. The simultaneous plucking of two strings might require some adjustment in terms of coordination, begin by just combining a thumb stroke with index, middle, and ring fingers plucking if needed.

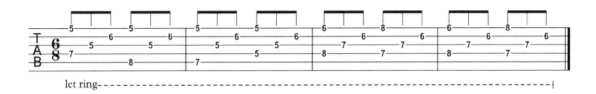

Asking Questions

Level: Intermediate

Techniques: Fingerstyle

Description: Open strings can serve to generate interesting intervals when combined with fingered pitches up the neck. Use this ethereal sounding progression to develop your finger coordination when arpeggiating. If you want to focus solely on the plucking hand, pick an interesting static voicing and arpeggiate it with all different finger permutations in your plucking hand.

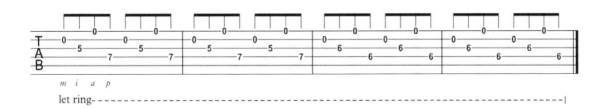

A Drop in The Bucket

Description: This finger-twisting chord progression challenges your endurance and ability to seamlessly transition between intricate voicings. It's constructed upon various inversions of Drop 2+4 voicings on the top four strings; these type of chords are a great way to spice up your comping, arpeggios, and even soloing, inserting intervals you wouldn't find in close position voicings.

Wait, I'm Confused

Description: This melodic line features the occasional use of two distinct voices, and requires some dexterity to be properly executed. It encompasses several fingerstyle techniques, providing a well-rounded workout to insert in your routine.

Ghostly Rhythms

Level: Advanced

Techniques: Strumming

Description: Speed bursts are a great way to improve relaxation in your wrist, and can also serve a musical purpose when playing in a funk rhythm setting. The infamous ghosted 32nds can breathe life into the most static of lines, but they are quite tricky to accurately execute.

A good starting tempo would be half of what you'd be comfortable with if you were playing constant 16th notes. Ensure precise articulation of every note, and maintain a constant tempo throughout the task.

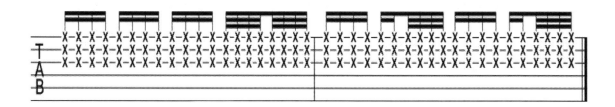

Chapter #9

A Few Fun Exercises

- I play guitar because it lets me dream out loud. – Michael Hedges.

Now that you have gone through all the tiring repetitive drills, let's end the book with a few fun musical exercises. You may look at these as more of musical compositions than exercises. I am sure you will enjoy it!

Have fun!

Vibin' In Detroit

Category: Picking Hand
Level: Beginner
Techniques: Strumming

Description: This simple Motown inspired chord progression could prove to be a feat in endurance. Remember: the right hand is the engine of the player, make sure to outline every 16th subdivision by hovering your picking hand above the strings over the rests, and make those ghost notes pop out!

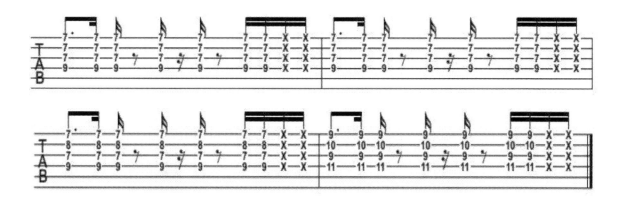

Impending Doom

Category: Picking Hand		
Level: Beginner		
Techniques: Downpicking		

Description: A punishing 80s Thrash Metal riff constructed to obliterate your picking hand. Downpick every note, while maintaining a clear and percussive articulation. Even though it's an aggressive riff, try not to tense up and keep a relaxed wrist and pick grip.

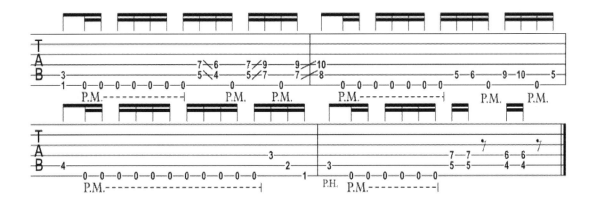

Chunky Riff

Category: Fretting & Picking Hand		
Level: Intermediate		
Techniques: Downpicking, Palm Muting		

Description: an 80s reminiscent riff, optimal for training your downpicking and palm muting skills. Highlight the tonal differences between the more percussive muted parts and the resonant chords.

A

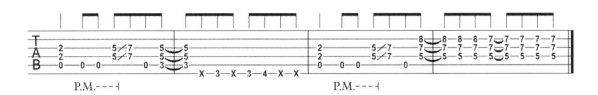

B

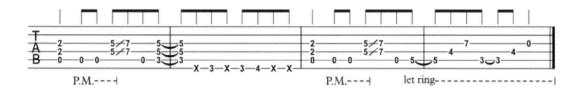

Picking Drill

Category: Picking Hand
Level: Intermediate
Techniques: Economy + Alternate Picking

Description: A folk flavoured rock riff, will do wonders for your picking technique. This could be approach in a number of ways, try to economise motion by always using a downstroke when ascending and an upstroke when descending, but be aware of how the pattern shifts and maybe incorporate alternate picking to rectify it before landing on the next 1.

A

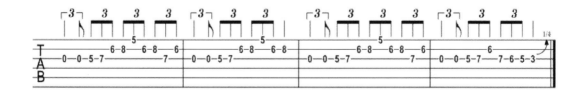

B

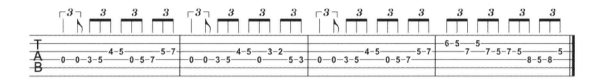

Oh, I Wonder

Category: Fretting & Picking Hand

Level: Advanced

Techniques: Two-Handed Tapping, Legato, Slide

Description: This odd-metered melodic line presents a variety of techniques to be employed, without having to pick a single note! Use the hammer-ons from nowhere technique to attack the notes with the left hand, and you index or middle finger to tap with your right hand.

Slides executed with the tapping finger can be tricky, make sure to master them at slower tempos before increasing it.

A

B

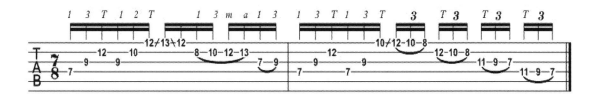

Until Next Time!

That brings us to the end of the book. I had a lot of fun writing the book and I hope it's same with you too. I hope I was able to add value and help your guitar playing. If yes, could you please leave a review for the book on amazon? Reviews are the lifeblood of books and I need as many as I can to reach as many people as possible.

Here's a link to leave a review:

http://bit.ly/guitarreview

Thank you again for selecting my book. Hope to see you soon with another book.

Like my Facebook page for fun guitar content. Also, send me a video of you playing your favorite exercise from the book and I will feature it on the page.

www.facebook.com/theguitarhead/.

THE END